EXAMINING POLITICAL SYSTEMS™

THEOCRACY

Henrietta Toth

rosen publishing's
rosen central®
New York

For my niece Emi

Published in 2020 by The Rosen Publishing Group, Inc.
29 East 21st Street, New York, NY 10010

First Edition

Library of Congress Cataloging-in-Publication Data

Names: Toth, Henrietta, author.
Title: Theocracy / Henrietta Toth.
Description: First edition. | New York : Rosen Central, 2020. | Series: Examining political systems | Includes bibliographical references and index. | Audience: Grades 5–8.
Identifiers: LCCN 2018016951| ISBN 9781508185567 (library bound) | ISBN 9781508185550 (pbk.)
Subjects: LCSH: Theocracy—Juvenile literature.
Classification: LCC JC372 .T68 2019 | DDC 321/.5—dc23
LC record available at https://lccn.loc.gov/2018016951

Manufactured in the United States of America

On the cover: Pope Francis greets pilgrims in St. Peter's Square in Vatican City, Rome (*top*), and Muslim women pray on the floor of a mosque in Aceh, Indonesia (*bottom*). The Bible (background) has been a foundational text for Christian and Jewish theocracies.

CONTENTS

INTRODUCTION

Theocracy is a type of government that has been in use for many millennia. Its roots are found in several ancient civilizations, from the Egyptians in North Africa to the Mayans in Central America. The term "theocracy" comes from the Greek word *theokratia*, which means to be ruled by God. Jewish historian Flavius Josephus (37–100 CE) coined the term in about 100 CE to describe the government of the kingdoms of Israel.

The political system or type of government called theocracy is based on a religious deity, whose worship holds the highest power in matters of the state and in life. Civic rulers govern in the name of God or a supreme being. Some theocratic rulers claim to have divine right and receive divine guidance. These rulers include kings, making a theocracy also a monarchy. In other theocracies, the rulers belong to a religious order, such as the pope in Roman Catholic Christianity and the supreme leader in Islam.

In a theocracy, the legal system is based on religious law, meaning the country's laws are determined and dictated by religion. For example, in Iran sharia law, which is based on Islam, governs daily life. Some view theocratic governments as tyrannical. Personal freedoms are regulated, especially as they relate to religious law. Citizens must conform to a society ruled by the teachings of a holy book or religious texts.

Theocracies are one of various forms of government practiced throughout human history. Early civilizations were commonly governed

A group of Muslim boys study the Quran in a reading class at a mosque in central Baghdad, Iraq, during the holy fasting month of Ramadan.

by theocratic rule. There are examples of early theocracies in the major religions of Christianity, Islam, and Judaism. Some of America's colonial settlers lived in a theocratic society. The Puritans came to Massachusetts Bay Colony in the 1630s. Leaders of the colony demanded a rigid following of Protestant Christianity, with harsh discipline of those settlers who failed to apply it to their daily lives. In about 1776, the first Mennonites arrived in Upper Canada. This conservative Protestant group practiced a type of theocracy through the traditional observance of their faith.

Today, theocracy is rarely practiced. However, modern theocracies exist in Africa and the Middle East. Islamic theocracies are the governing structures in countries like Afghanistan, Iran, and Saudi Arabia. The Vatican in Rome is an example of a Catholic theocracy. In the United States and Israel, groups with extreme religious views seek to promote a more conservative and repressive society. Theocracy's ancient roots are now reaching into the future as new forms of this type of government are on the rise.

CHAPTER 1

THE ROOTS OF THEOCRACY

Historically, theocracy is an uncommon form of government. Yet, it is a very old form of rule, whose roots run deep in the history of mankind. Theocracy arose around 3100 BCE in societies where the majority of citizens followed the same religion. Moral and social issues were enforced by the government to conform to the common faith. Rulers of theocracies were believed to have a direct connection with the religion and its god. The Bible says that God, or Yahweh, chose Moses to lead the Hebrews. Moses, unsure of his abilities to lead, responded, "Oh, my Lord, send, I pray, some other person."

Moses Drawing Water from the Rock depicts the prophet leading the Israelites. This oil painting was created by the Italian artist known as Tintoretto in 1577.

THE EARLY HEBREWS AND THEOCRACY

In about 1300 BCE, the early Hebrews practiced a form of theocracy under the prophet Moses. God was the head of his people and his word was the law. Faith and religion played the primary role in a government and society that followed the laws of the Bible. The Old Testament called Moses "a man of God," with whom Moses had a direct connection. Moses governed

MOSES AND THE TEN COMMANDMENTS

History traditionally states that Moses (ca. 1391–ca. 1271 BCE) grew up as the adopted son of an Egyptian princess. He became an important prophet and leader of the Jewish people in place of God. According to the Bible, Moses represented God, spoke directly with him, and relayed his instructions to his people. Through Moses, God revealed the Ten Commandments, which were inscribed on stone tablets. The Ten Commandments listed standards by which to live. They are divided into directions on how to treat God and how to treat fellow human beings. The commandments about God instruct followers to worship him exclusively, not to form idols in place of him, not to misuse his name, and to set aside the seventh day of the week for worship. The commandments about how to treat others are to treat one's parents with honor and to not murder, commit adultery, steal, tell falsehoods about others, or covet (envy) what other people possess.

The Ten Commandments are important principles in Judaism and Christianity. Moses is regarded as a major prophet in the religions of Judaism, Christianity, and Islam.

the Hebrews on behalf of God, who instructed him to lead them out of slavery from Egypt. This directive was given to Moses as a divine revelation in the form of a burning bush located on Mount Horeb.

By 1200 BCE, the Hebrews were governed by judges, who ruled as representatives of Yahweh, or God. A monarchy followed, in which kings were believed to be God's divine servants.

HOW THEOCRACIES AROSE

Theocracies arose in those communities and city-states where the majority of the population believed in one God or group of gods, like in ancient Egypt. More specifically, theocracies flourished in societies where people believed that God was directly concerned with their lives and their conduct. God or the deity was considered the head of state who ruled on earth through a human spokesperson.

Religion and the god or deity were the source of all authority. A country's government and its laws and regulations were based on the religion that the majority of the people followed. The laws of church and state were not separate but were combined. The sacred texts of the religion—the Bible, Quran, and Book of Mormon—were viewed as coming directly from God. Their purpose was to develop the laws and rules by which to govern a society.

HOW THEOCRATIC LEADERS RULED

Rulers of theocratic civilizations maintained control and command by claiming the divine right to govern. They claimed their authority came from a specific belief system or direct communication with God or a deity. Thus, theocratic rulers declared their power over all citizens in the name of God or a deity. These rulers interpreted the religious texts and claimed to follow the will of God for all people based on their common religion. First, rulers were to serve God and their religion and then the people. However, these leaders could also interpret the religious texts for political reasons, including to benefit themselves, and rule as a monarch or a dictator.

Some theocratic rulers claimed descent from the deity, thus making them living gods on earth. Others claimed they were given the divine right to be messengers of God on earth. Moses delivered God's message of the Ten Commandments to the Israelites, and Muhammad brought the Quran to the Muslims. Sacred scriptures were accepted as messages from God.

Most leaders inherited their rule, like the pharaohs, or they were chosen to govern by previous leaders. Usually there were no limits on the length of time that a leader could rule.

VIEWS ON THEOCRACY

Theocracy is viewed in different ways by people in different nations. Culture and religion both influence beliefs or attitudes on theocracy. People of nations with long histories of theocracy view this form of government as having more pros than cons. Other societies, especially Western countries, see more cons than pros in a theocracy.

PROS OF A THEOCRACY

A positive aspect of theocracy is that it encourages social unity because all of a country's inhabitants believe in one god and ruler. There is only one faith that is followed by all citizens within that country. For example, all inhabitants of Saudi Arabia must be Muslims who believe in Allah. With one religion, there can be no arguing or opposing views on faith or religious observances.

MUHAMMAD AND THE QURAN

Muhammad ibn Abdullah (ca. 570–632 CE) was a merchant living in Mecca, in today's Saudi Arabia, who founded Islam. Like Moses, Muhammad was a messenger and prophet who conveyed God's, or Allah's, words to his people. Beginning in 609 CE, Muhammad experienced several divine revelations in which the angel Gabriel revealed the words of God to him. These revelations form the core of the Quran, Islam's holy book. The Quran discloses the "nature of God," or what God is about, and also lays down the rules by which God expects Muslims to live and worship. *Islam* in Arabic means "surrender." Followers of Islam surrender to the will of God and observe strict religious practices.

This page from an eighth-century manuscript of the Quran was written on parchment. It is in the collection of the Los Angeles County Museum.

Some political scholars believe that a theocratic government is more efficient. They see decision making as more organized and productive. Within a theocratic government, there is no legislative branch, so new laws are often quickly enacted. In Islamic countries, laws are developed based on the country's constitution, which follows religious sharia laws. Strict enforcement of these laws results in less crime because people may fear the harsh punishments, such as flogging and stoning, that can be imposed.

Women wearing hijabs sit on the steps near the shrine of the Islamic scholar Hazrat Abdul Azim Hasani in Tehran, Iran.

CONS OF A THEOCRACY

A negative aspect of theocracy is that it can foster an intolerance of other societies and their belief systems. It does not favorably view multicultural societies and often puts limits on contact with other and different groups of people. Social progress and embracing new ideas are often restricted. A theocratic society can pose a threat to civil and religious liberties. Citizens also may be limited in their abilities to defend and express themselves. Writers and artists have their works censored and are often threatened. Women have different rights in a theocracy, like having their dress monitored. In many Islamic theocracies, women are required to wear a hijab or chador that completely covers their bodies.

In a theocratic government, the ruler can wield too much power. This can occur because the government lacks different branches that keep checks and balances in place. Therefore, a powerful leader can abuse his authority and the people he rules. However, if a theocratic ruler suddenly becomes unable to lead, society and the country could become paralyzed and unable to function.

EARLY THEOCRACIES

Before her sacrificial death, a thirteen-year-old Inca girl known as Maiden was prepared for the ceremonial ritual by being given a special diet and offered drugs and alcohol. Maiden is an example of a human sacrifice that was sometimes made by ancient theocracies. These belief systems evolved over the centuries as smaller religious communities folded into larger civilizations. Government and religion were combined, and one did not exist without the other.

ANCIENT CULTURES

The earliest example of theocracy appeared five thousand years ago. The ancient theocratic Egyptians prospered for three thousand years. Theocracy was also practiced among the early Greeks and Romans and in Mesopotamia, which comprises present-day Iraq, Kuwait, and parts of Syria and Turkey. The united functions of religion and government were seen as bringing order to society. All aspects of government—such as the development of laws, construction of buildings, defense of the country, and trade with neighboring civilizations—were subject to religious rules.

EGYPT

The long period of ancient Egyptian history is divided into three kingdoms—Old, Middle, and New. History in Egypt began after the upper and lower parts of the country were unified into a single civilization. With the beginning of the Old Kingdom (ca. 2686–2160 BCE), a strong and well-organized theocratic government and society developed under the rule of kings, or pharaohs, which lasted through thirty dynasties.

The Egyptians practiced polytheism, or the worship of many gods. They worshipped about two thousand gods and goddesses. Many were gods of nature, who also held political power. Ra, the sun god, held a place of prominence. The pharaoh was seen as a living god and the supreme leader, who ruled by divine law. Next in command was the vizier or head priest, followed by administrators and district governors.

RAMSES THE GREAT

Ramses II (ca. 1303–1213 BCE) was recognized as the most powerful ancient theocratic ruler. His reign spanned sixty-seven years. He was also the most famous pharaoh, who worked at projecting his image as a larger-than-life leader. This is evidenced by the monuments he built to himself, such as the Great Temple of Abu Simbel. The temple included four huge statues of Ramses II himself in front. He built many other architectural masterpieces and signed the world's first peace treaty in recorded history with the Hittites, the ancient people of modern-day Turkey. Ramses II had several wives and claimed to have fathered more than one hundred children. Today his mummified remains have been autopsied and exhibited several times.

The Great Pyramids of Giza were built as tombs during the Old Kingdom as evidence of the pharaoh's great power. The pharaohs were often depicted as mighty warriors on the tombs' walls. The tombs were filled with necessities for the afterlife so that the mummified pharaohs could intercede with the gods on behalf of their former subjects.

In the Middle Kingdom (2181–1786 BCE), the pharaoh's rule as a god lessened. Instead, the pharaoh was seen as a manifestation of the gods sent to earth to guide their people. Also, members of the noble class began to exert their power, and the priests grew in number.

This view of the Giza pyramid complex shows the six various-sized structures, including the colossal Great Pyramid of Khufu, located outside the capital city of Cairo, Egypt.

CHINA

The Shang dynasty ruled China as a strong theocracy from 1600 to 1046 BCE. It was headed by an emperor, whose main role was religious. The Chinese ruler was seen as a son of heaven and a supreme deity. Rituals were commonly carried out and involved oracles, people or objects that could channel the responses of a god. Eventually, the emperor's role evolved into a ceremonial one, yet his words still held importance. In 1046 BCE, the Shang dynasty was overthrown, but it retained a courtly role and continued to carry out rituals.

The ruins of the ancient Inca city of Machu Picchu are located in the Andes Mountains of Peru. The city was built and occupied from the mid-fifteenth to about the mid-sixteenth centuries.

AZTEC, INCA, AND MAYA EMPIRES

The Aztec, Inca, and Maya civilizations were located in present-day Central and South America, the Yucatán, southern Mexico, northern Belize, and western Honduras. From 250 to 900 CE, their rulers were godlike kings, who were considered divine and powerful. Gods of nature were worshipped with human sacrifices. This practice showed their direct association with the gods. The mummy of the Inca girl called Maiden, sacrificed more than five hundred years ago, was found in 1999.

The Maya are the best known of the ancient civilizations of today's Central America. The Maya dynasty began in about 2600 BCE and ended in 1200 CE, when its people were integrated into the Toltec people. This advanced society contributed to the knowledge of astronomy and the calendar system. Like the Egyptians, they built pyramids and temples.

ANCIENT GREECE

Early Greek civilization was comprised of several independent city-states headed by kings. They made many artistic and intellectual contributions to history. The Greeks did not have a specific religion. Instead, they had a strong relationship with a dozen gods and goddesses, who they believed were aware of everything they did, provided for their needs, and protected them from their enemies, nature, and illness. The most powerful and important god was Zeus, god of weather and of justice. The well-being and safety of society depended on a good association with the gods. There was separation between this religion and the functions of the state. Those who disrespected the gods could be found guilty at trial and sentenced to death, as was the philosopher Socrates in 399 BCE. Priests and priestesses followed religious laws when conducting ceremonies and rituals.

THEOCRATIC WOMEN RULERS

The ancient Egyptian theocracy had a few powerful female leaders. The first woman pharaoh was Neithikret, who ruled from circa 2148 to 2144 BCE. She was not held in a positive light during her reign but was later remembered for her bravery and beauty. Sobeknefru governed next from circa 1787 to 1783 BCE. She is portrayed in artwork wearing the head cloth and kilt of a male pharaoh.

Egypt's most famous female pharaoh was Hatshepsut. She governed from about 1473 to 1458 BCE. Hatshepsut launched a military campaign and oversaw several grand building projects, including her burial temple. Two more female leaders—Nefertiti and Tawosret—ruled before the last and most famous pharaoh, Cleopatra VII, came to power. The close of her reign in 30 BCE marked the end of ancient Egypt.

ROMAN EMPIRE

The Roman Empire evolved in 27 BCE as an imperial power with great military and political success. Roman emperors governed as theocratic heads of state, who claimed to be descended from the gods who ruled through them, thus their power was seen as divine. During Rome's ancient period, the emperor was regarded as a deity until Christianity was brought in under Emperor Constantine I in 313 CE.

CALVINIST THEOCRACY

During the sixteenth century, the Protestant Reformation sought to reform the Catholic Church in Europe. Following the Protestant

This statue of Protestant leader John Calvin is part of the Reformation Wall, a monument to key figures of the Protestant Reformation. The statue was dedicated in 1909 in Geneva, Switzerland.

Reformation, there were several attempts to create theocracies. The best-known theocratic state was established by Protestant leader John Calvin (1509–1564) in Geneva, Switzerland. Calvin served as religious leader of the city of Geneva from 1536 to 1564. Calvin's Geneva was viewed by some as a divine "city of light set upon a hill."

Calvin advocated that society should give complete obedience to God and apply the religious scriptures to all civil and moral aspects of life. He believed that following the divine guidance and laws of God would unify society and elevate God's glory in the world. The theocratic stronghold of Geneva diminished after Calvin's death, as his followers slowly disbanded to other regions.

CHAPTER 3

THEOCRACY IN THE AGE OF ENLIGHTENMENT

On November 1, 1755, Christians celebrated All Saints' Day. That same Saturday morning, an earthquake destroyed the city of Lisbon, Portugal. A fire and a tsunami followed that killed more than forty thousand people. Theologians said God sent the catastrophe as divine retribution for the sins of mankind.

THE AGE OF REASON

For centuries, religion taught that God was directly responsible for world events. During the Enlightenment, philosophers argued that only nature could be blamed for disasters like an earthquake. Voltaire, a French philosopher, spoke out against the Catholic Church for claiming that God used such methods to punish his people.

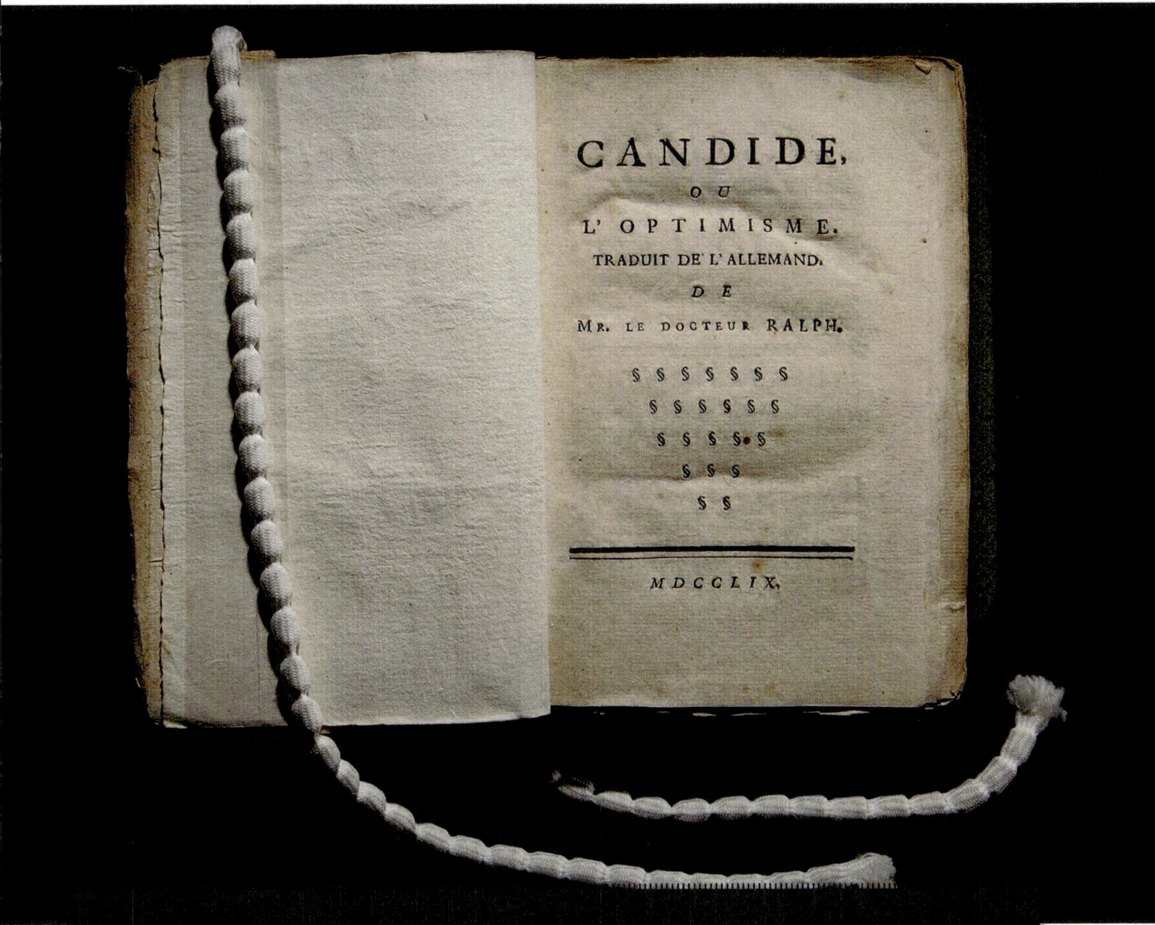

A 1759 copy of *Candide* by the French writer and philosopher Voltaire is displayed in the Voltaire Room at the University of Oxford in England.

The Enlightenment was an intellectual and philosophical movement that examined a wide range of issues. Also known as the Age of Reason, the movement spanned some two hundred years, from about 1600 to 1800. Philosophers and writers spoke and wrote on a variety of topics—from religion to medicine and science—which enlightened and educated the population. The great thinkers of the Enlightenment spread their ideas through their discussions with other philosophers, lectures, and writings.

In the Middle Ages, before the Age of Reason, kings governed by divine right. In places where there was no civil government, prince-bishops ruled and they could interpret the religion for civil purposes. Reform of religions and the wars fought over them paved the way for the Enlightenment. The movement advanced human progress by putting down the divine claims of rulers and the church. The philosophers suggested that people could rationalize about religion for themselves.

The Enlightenment had a large impact and lasting influence on society, especially the development of human thinking and culture. It led the way to the modern age, and the progress of

VOLTAIRE

Voltaire was the pen name of Francois-Marie Arouet (1694–1778), a French historian, philosopher, and writer of the Enlightenment. He is best known for promoting the separation of church and state and for advocating for the freedoms of religion and speech. In 1734, an arrest warrant was issued for him for his attack on the Catholic Church and established religion. Voltaire wrote essays, novels, plays, and poems about history, religion, science, and other topics that advocated for the progress of people. He produced more than twenty thousand letters and some two thousand books and pamphlets. His most famous work is the short novel *Candide*. It is a satire that pokes fun at the attitudes and events of the time as the main character Candide experiences them.

science evolved from these new ways of thinking. During the Age of Reason, philosophers advanced the necessity and right of personal liberty. They put forth that people should live their lives as they saw fit as long as they were being lawful. They also stated that government should not promote or interfere in religious matters and that freedom of religion formed the base of a liberal civilization.

THE DECLINE OF THEOCRACY

Theocratic ideals influenced most governments across the globe from the earliest time of recorded history until the Enlightenment. After the twelfth century, theocracies began to decline in most Western states and nations and the term "theocracy" began to take on a negative tone. Jewish historian Flavius Josephus had coined the term "theocracy" in about 100 CE, and his definition was first used in English to describe a government divinely inspired. By 1800, theocracy was defined as a government run by priests or religious groups that exerted political powers.

The Enlightenment had a direct effect on the decline of

A statue of the early Jewish historian Flavius Josephus stands at the entrance to the visitors' center at the Masada Museum near the ancient Masada fortress in Israel.

This oil portrait of English philosopher and physician John Locke was painted in 1697 by the leading English portrait painter Sir Godfrey Kneller. It is in the collection of the Hermitage Museum in St. Petersburg, Russia.

theocracy when it came to be recognized as contradictory to liberal thought. It was rejected for its outmoded methods and violation of human rights. Influential figures of the Enlightenment promoted a stand against the authoritarian nature of theocratic governments and the manner by which they controlled society. Instead, Enlightenment thinkers advocated for the development of societies based on human rights, thus becoming more democratic. This new and enlightened view of government and society found a footing in the English Reformation, when the church broke from the Roman Catholic Church. It also influenced the revolutions in the American colonies and in France.

Before the Age of Reason, theorists in England had supported the divine right of kings to rule. English philosopher John Locke disagreed and stated that God's word could be interpreted by mankind in different ways, saying, "Revelation must be judged by reason."

RELIGION IN THE AGE OF ENLIGHTENMENT

By the time of the Enlightenment, views on religion had changed. Religion came to be seen as the only business in which the church should be involved. Government was a distinctly separate body.

English philosopher John Locke drew a line between church and state by saying that religion was of an "inward persuasion" and government and its officials were of an "outward force." Locke believed that civil peace depended on separating the interests of the church, which he saw as "private," and the "public" interests of the state. He said government should be wholly secular and unaffected by religious devotion. Locke saw allegiance to the state as a requirement and the church as a "voluntary society of men."

JOHN LOCKE

John Locke (1632–1704) was a philosopher and a physician. In his childhood, his family belonged to the Church of England, but its members were supportive of the Puritan cause. This early view of religion influenced Locke's later thinking and works on government, religion, and personal identity. At the University of Oxford, Locke excelled at his studies and sought contact with the leading thinkers of his time. In 1689, Locke produced his major philosophical work, *Two Treatises of Government*, about the political situation in England. Locke's writings laid the groundwork for the intellectual development of the Western world. His influence can be seen in the Declaration of Independence and the US Constitution.

Voltaire recognized a difference between "state religion" and "theological religion." He wrote, "A state religion can never cause turmoil. This is not true of theological religion; it is the source of all the follies and turmoil imaginable; it is the mother of fanaticism and civil discord; it is the enemy of mankind."

The Enlightenment also generated new beliefs about religion. The philosophers suggested that in earlier civilizations God helped people of limited education and understanding grasp religion by providing stories and miraculous events. Now there was a move away from being obsessed with the miraculous. People could reason for themselves about religion. Leaders of the Enlightenment still recognized the importance of established religion and a church to morally guide the population, as long as it was voluntary and without force. They believed in the existence of a God who was indirectly involved with the world, and they rejected the claim of kings to rule by divine right. The philosophers also advocated for the tolerance of different religions and the freedom for people to worship as they wished.

THE RISE OF NATIONALISM

The Enlightenment saw the rise of nationalism and the view of the nation as a political religion. The state or nation became more important than the church or God. The nation was seen as something real versus religion that was of the supernatural. Loyalty and devotion to the nation gathered more significance, especially in times of conflict or war. Dying for one's nation was not in vain. Patriotism and nationalism could bring people together regardless of the religion they practiced or disagreement or hostility between religions.

CHAPTER 4

THEOCRACY IN AMERICA

Some of America's earliest settlements began as theocracies. However, more than 150 years later, America's Founding Fathers advocated for the separation of church and state. John Adams noted the new government's intention by saying "the United States is not, in any sense, founded on the Christian religion."

Pilgrims Going to Church is an oil painting that depicts the harsh living conditions of the early settlers in the New World. American artist George Henry Boughton painted the winter scene in 1867.

EARLY NEW ENGLAND

The Pilgrims and Puritans were Protestants who followed the teachings of John Calvin.

The Pilgrims separated from the Church of England, while the Puritans tried to "purify" the church from Catholic rituals and conducted simple services. The Church of England had broken away from the Roman Catholic Church in 1534.

In 1620, the Pilgrims arrived in Plymouth Bay, Massachusetts. They were a pious group who believed in forgiving others. They also believed it was their right to occupy and settle land in the New World. The English king's patent, or license, gave them title to the land without purchasing it from the Native Americans.

JOHN WINTHROP

John Winthrop (1588–1649) was the first governor and leading founder of the Massachusetts Bay Colony. In his early adulthood, he was a country squire and lawyer in England. From a young age, Winthrop was highly religious. He became a Puritan who saw the world as wicked and in need of being remade. King Charles I's anti-Puritan policies prompted Winthrop to join the Massachusetts Bay Company, which sought to establish a colony in New England. He was elected governor of the new colony and sailed to the New World in 1630. When the colonists later decided they wanted representation in making decisions, Winthrop became irritated. Roger Williams was especially critical of this relationship between church and state and in 1636 he fled to Rhode Island—with the secret help of Winthrop.

In 1630, one thousand Puritan refugees fled religious persecution in England to found the Massachusetts Bay Colony. Led by Governor John Winthrop, they established a theocratic rule limited to church members. Their goal was to be led by Christ working through ministers who followed God's will. Only men who could prove their worthiness were appointed to lead. The Puritans sought to create a model biblical city, "a City upon a Hill," and saw it as their manifest destiny to settle New England. Control over the growing population was achieved by demanding strict observances of "religious belief and practices," and "dissenters" could be hanged.

Theocracy in the community of Salem, Massachusetts, had a direct and profound effect on the witchcraft trials held there between 1692 and 1693. Punishment for witchcraft included stoning, or being killed by being pelted with stones, a punishment sometimes used in Middle Eastern theocracies today.

LIFE IN A PURITAN THEOCRACY

In a Puritan theocracy, life and society was managed by "godly rule" for the "common good," according to Governor Winthrop. Religious thought was controlled and certain activities were monitored. The sale of alcohol was regulated, while card playing and

Colonial governor John Winthrop influenced the development of early New England. His seventeenth-century oil portrait was painted by Sir Anthony Van Dyck.

smoking were banned. However, the Massachusetts code of laws contained some democratic principles for the time period. It prohibited slavery and cruelty to children, wives, servants, and farm animals.

EARLY VIRGINIA

The Church of England played a dominant role in the colony of Virginia. Attendance at services was compulsory, and anyone not complying with this law or criticizing the church could have his or her property confiscated. The church also enforced civil matters, such as levying taxes. In the neighboring colony of Maryland, a seventeenth-century law made it a capital offense to deny the divinity of Jesus Christ. When the American Revolution began, people found it difficult to belong to a church that was headed by the king of England.

ROGER WILLIAMS

Roger Williams (ca. 1603–1683) was a religious leader and the founder of Rhode Island, serving as its first president. He arrived in Boston from England in 1631 and bounced around settlements in the Massachusetts Bay Colony. Eventually, Williams wore out his welcome with his differing views on civil and religious matters and was banished from the colony by the authorities. Williams fled to Rhode Island, establishing that colony on the basis of religious freedom and the separation of church and state. In 1644, Williams advocated for a "hedge or wall of separation between the garden of the church and the wilderness of the world."

LATER THEOCRATIC GROUPS

Smaller theocratic groups later emigrated to or sprung up in the United States. They shared the common thread of theocracy, but each group implemented it differently. However, they continue to share in the long-term success of their religious governing that has continued into the modern age.

AMISH

The Amish were founded in the Germanic states of Europe in the late seventeenth century. In the nineteenth and twentieth

Mormons emigrating west guide their covered wagons through Echo Canyon near Salt Lake City, Utah. This circa 1870 photograph was taken by Charles William Carter.

centuries, they emigrated to North America. The Amish believe in the separation of church and state and also in being detached from the world. Their daily life, including their dress, is governed by a code of behavior. Some very strict Amish orders do not use electricity or electronics. Bishops and preachers lead the Amish in meetings held in the homes of members.

MORMONS

The Church of Jesus Christ of Latter-day Saints, or Mormons, was founded in the 1820s by Joseph Smith in upstate New York. Smith claimed the angel Moroni revealed gold tablets to him inscribed with the text that became the Book of Mormon. In the 1840s, the Mormons moved to the Utah Territory to escape persecution for some of their practices, including polygamy.

In the 1880s, statehood for Utah was delayed when leaders in Washington noted that "Utah has a theocratic government while other states and territories have republican governments, the church being supreme over all." Local legislators worked at reducing Utah's theocratic ways in order for it to finally gain statehood in 1896. The group follows the Book of Mormon and rules by theodemocracy, "a government of God and good men."

SATMARS

The Satmars are a branch of Hasidic Jews founded in Hungary in 1905 by Rabbi Joel Teitelbaum. The rapidly growing group established itself in New York after World War II. A grand rabbi leads the Satmars in spiritual matters. Daily life—including customs, dress, and language—follows a biblical code of religious uniformity.

The Satmars founded the village of Kiryas Joel in New York in 1977 as an insular theocratic community. Signs posted at the town's entrances ask visitors to follow their "traditions and religious customs," including "wearing long skirts or pants, covered necklines, and sleeves past the elbow." In 2017, residents voted to create a separate town government to have power over zoning and other issues. One voter expressed how the group works under religious leaders: "We tend to follow the majority and they wanted it. They know the ins and outs of what's good for the village and so I voted for it."

JEHOVAH'S WITNESSES

In 1872, the Jehovah's Witnesses was founded in Pittsburgh, Pennsylvania, by Charles Taze Russell. This evangelistic group is led by a president. Jehovah's Witnesses emphasize separation of religion from secular government and cite biblical reasons for not engaging in military service and refusing blood transfusions. Holidays, such as Christmas and Easter, are considered remnants of pagan rituals and are not celebrated. Members limit their association with non–Jehovah's Witnesses. They believe that the end of the world is nearing, which will bring God's rule over all.

CHAPTER 5

CONTEMPORARY THEOCRACIES

In Iran, women begin to wear a hijab or chador at thirteen years of age. Iran is a theocracy where this ancient custom has been required of women since 1979. Theocracy is old and yet new, as today there are about a dozen theocratic nations in the world. Most embrace the Islamic faith and follow the Quran, Islam's holy text. The official language of many Islamic countries is Arabic.

THEOCRACY IN THE MODERN AGE

Since Muhammad founded Islam in the seventh century, it has become a major world religion with more than 1.5 billion Muslims. The founding of Islam was based on no distinction made between religious and civil power. Islamic states operate with religion as their base, but they really function as political systems. The leader or religious group acts in the place of a civil government. If a civil government is also present, it must submit to the dictates of religious leaders. Most Islamic countries are theocratic republics, a cross between a theocracy and a republic. In theory, they are theocracies but still republics whose laws must be consistent with Islam.

In the modern day, theocracy has gained a foothold in countries where only Islam is practiced and all citizens are Muslims. Islamic fundamentalists seek to create a theocratic society as it existed in the days under Muhammad. Most of these theocracies are in the Middle East and parts of Africa, Asia, and Europe.

AFGHANISTAN

Afghanistan had a secular government from 1978 until 1992. The Taliban came to rule from 1996 until 2001. It is now an Islamic country and a theocracy. The Quran is interpreted to unify the

A large crowd of men take part in a rally held by the Taliban in October 1996 in Kabul, the capital city of Afghanistan.

Afghan society in strict accordance with Islam and the will of God. Government and society adhere to the sharia law of Islam. Afghan fundamentalist religious leaders or clerics have ultimate political control.

IRAN

The shah, or king, once ruled the Islamic Republic of Iran as a secular country. From 1924 until 1979, extreme expressions of Islam were outlawed, including the hijab and chador. The shah was overthrown during the Iranian Revolution in 1979, and a fundamentalist supreme leader came to power. Iran's constitution states that the supreme leader—who is a scholar of Islam—can best interpret Islam and ensure that the people follow the strict religious practices prescribed in the Quran. He wields the most influence in the country and even has approval over the elected position of the president. The supreme leader appoints military leaders, governmental heads, and directors of television and radio stations.

Iran's legal system follows the religious sharia laws. Every sector, from the military to finance to civil laws, are affected. Religious courts determine if sharia law is being followed appropriately and morality police enforce rules of dress and behavior. Following Islamic law is viewed as unifying and controlling society, as well as keeping Muslims safe and on the spiritual path to Allah.

MAURITANIA

The Islamic Republic of Mauritania is a small country in western North Africa. It was under a Western-style rule as a territory of France until 1960. By 1980, a new government instituted theocratic rule that strictly adheres to sharia law.

AYATOLLAH RUHOLLAH KHOMEINI

Ayatollah Ruhollah Khomeini (1900–1989) was the supreme leader of Iran from 1979 until 1989. From an early age, Khomeini studied Islam and wrote about Islamic ethics, law, and philosophy. By 1950, he was recognized as a major religious and political leader. In 1964, Khomeini was exiled from Iran for speaking out against the shah's rule and Western influences in Iran, and for advocating Islamic purity. Khomeini returned to Iran in February 1979. He assumed power after his supporters helped force out the shah during the Iranian Revolution.

Men carry a poster of the Islamic cleric Ayatollah Ruhollah Khomeini during a demonstration against the shah of Iran in the capital city of Tehran, Iran, in 1979.

SAUDI ARABIA

Saudi Arabia is a theocracy and a monarchy ruled by the House of Saud since 1932. The king leads by divine right and power. The government is tightly controlled and the constitution strictly abides by the Quran. Sharia law is enforced by the religious police force. Two of Islam's holiest sites—Mecca and Medina—are in Saudi Arabia. No religion other than Islam is allowed and all inhabitants must be Muslims. Anyone who promotes another religion or insults Islam can be severely punished, even with death.

SUDAN

The Republic of the Sudan is located in northern Africa. It is headed by a president and the constitution is based on the Quran. The national anthem proclaims, "We are the Soldiers of God, the Soldiers of the Nation." The Sudanese government operates under sharia laws so the population, which is 97 percent Muslim, must conform to the sharia Islamic legal system. Offenses can be punished by stoning to death.

VATICAN CITY

The Vatican City, also known as the Holy See, is a Catholic theocracy. It was formally founded in 1929 in Rome on 100 acres (40 hectares), although it has been around since earlier Christian times. The pope governs Vatican City as well as the Catholic Church and answers only to God. He is viewed as a representative of God, but not as a prophet who receives direct communication. The pope oversees all moral and religious values in civic affairs and has the final say in all matters. Elected by the College of Cardinals, the pope serves as leader until he

Pope Francis arrives in St. Peter's Square in Vatican City, Rome, for his weekly general audience with pilgrims and visitors who come to see him and receive his blessing.

dies or resigns. It is the only theocracy that elects a ruler instead of appointing one, and the position cannot be inherited.

The Vatican is recognized as a sovereign and independent state. The pope appoints members of the clergy to state positions to oversee the Vatican's diplomatic relations with other nations. Vatican City's legal system is based on the canon law of the Catholic Church. Its own police force protects the almost one thousand residents, while a separate guard protects the pope. The Vatican is an independent economy with its own bank.

YEMEN

The Republic of Yemen is situated on the southern portion of the Arabian Peninsula. As an Islamic country, its government is rooted in sharia law headed by a president. Yemen is a poor and developing country caught in political conflict and civil war, resulting in a population in need of humanitarian aid.

LIVING IN A THEOCRACY

Life in a contemporary theocracy means living in a society closed off from the greater world. Contact with other countries is regulated and even restricted. Religious laws affect everyday life and are enforced for dress, jobs, and travel, among other things. The availability of goods must adhere to religious laws. The content of television and radio stations, newspapers, books, magazines, and the internet is controlled and monitored to adhere to the will of God. Women and minorities, such as the LGBT community, are subject to harsh scrutiny, laws, and punishment. Judgment and punishment for offenses against religious laws are severe and are believed to come from a divine source.

Special regulations are imposed on women. Education is limited by age or even prohibited in some theocracies. When the Taliban came to power in Afghanistan in 1996, it forbade education for girls over age nine and prohibited women from being teachers. The Taliban claimed that limiting education was best for women and conformed with the teachings of Islam.

In a theocracy, women may not be able to pursue certain jobs and activities. In Saudi Arabia, women are just now allowed to drive. In many theocracies, women are required to wear a hijab or chador. According to the Quran, this modest form of dress expresses their faith and devotion to the Muslim way of life.

CHAPTER 6

NEW FORMS OF THEOCRACY

On November 4, 1979, Iranian students stormed the American Embassy in Tehran, Iran, and took fifty-two hostages. The students were supporters of the Iranian Revolution, which lasted from January 1978 until April 1, 1979, when the shah's

During the Iranian hostage crisis, Iranian students march a blindfolded American hostage across the embassy grounds in front of the international media on November 11, 1979.

monarchy was toppled. Iran was now an Islamic republic led by Supreme Leader Ruhollah Khomeini. It was a new theocracy in the modern age.

THE RETURN OF THEOCRACY

If theocracy has its roots in ancient civilizations, can it branch out into the modern world? What is the future of theocracy in today's societies? Some modern cultures have reembraced this form of government. And new forms of theocracy are emerging or are on the verge of being implemented in the twenty-first century.

In ancient times, people obeyed and trusted the pharaohs and kings to lead them. In modern times, people elect or have thrust upon them political or religious leaders whom they must trust without question to lead them in all affairs of faith and government.

Theocracy has developed into many forms throughout its existence. Monarchs throughout history, such as King James I, have put forth their divine association as evidence of their right and ability to rule. The monarch of England, as the head of the Church of England, blurs the line between church and state.

THEOCRACY TODAY

Of the world's nearly two hundred countries, just ten are governed as true theocracies. Nine of these nations are Islamic, while one, the Vatican, is Christian. In the twenty-first century, movements to bring back theocracy have been rising. Muslim fundamentalists have sought to establish conservative theocracies in Algeria, Egypt, Iraq, Pakistan, Somalia, Sudan, Turkey, and other countries where Islam is practiced. Theocratic tribes exist in Africa and Asia. The Central Tibetan Administration has functioned as a Buddhist theocracy.

Ultra-Orthodox Jews gather for the funeral of Rabbi Shmuel Auerbach in Jerusalem in February 2018. The rabbi had led a small group of followers who opposed more mainstream ultra-Orthodox Judaism.

Fundamentalist Christian groups have also tried to establish aspects of a theocracy in the United States, Canada, and Australia. In rural parts of Canada, some groups are embracing theocratic thinking with a conservative outlook. They say that the Canadian Charter of Rights and Freedoms allows for the expression of individual interpretations of faith and moral behavior.

In Israel, ultra-Orthodox Jewish sects have pushed for a return to the theocratic rule of biblical times. Israel was founded in 1947 as a secular state, but the pressure increases to revert to a theocracy.

The new forms of theocracy rising in the twenty-first century come on the heels of communism's defeat and are seen as a threat to civic and religious freedoms, as well as human rights. Radical religion is rising in the Middle East. Terrorism is used by groups such as the Taliban and Islamic State of Iraq and Syria (ISIS) to advance theocratic ideals.

THEOCRACY IN AMERICA?

Could theocracy take root in modern America? Theocracy is opposed to Western, and especially American, ideals. These include the United States' founding as a multicultural society with freedom of religion, as promoted by the country's founders. The fourth US president, James Madison, is considered the father of the US Constitution. Madison recognized the discord that a theocracy could create, especially if religious leaders used their position to advance political ideas. It could threaten personal liberty if civil and religious powers were linked, he warned. Madison promoted the separation of church and state.

Madison and other writers of the US Constitution were influenced by the philosophers of the Enlightenment. The basis of the Constitution is secular and states that the people "ordain and establish this Constitution for the United States of America." The Constitution does not advocate for one religion over another. Ratified in 1791, the First Amendment of the document states that "Congress shall make no law respecting an establishment of religion, or prohibiting the free exercise thereof; or abridging the freedom of speech, or of the press; or the right of the people peaceably to assemble, and to petition the Government for a redress of grievances."

This is the first page of the Constitution of the United States, which was created during the Constitutional Convention in 1787. The document is in the National Archives in Washington, DC. See partial transcription on page 53.

THEOCRACY VERSUS DEMOCRACY

The Puritans have had a lingering effect on religion in the United States since they arrived on its shores three centuries ago. They set the tone for the Protestant ethic of conservatism and hard work from which some religious groups say American culture has drifted. There are Christian fundamentalist groups who want to desecularize the country and promote a modern theocracy with Christianity as the national religion.

One of these groups is the religious right, which leans toward extreme conservatism. Its members would like a government that enacts political and social change based on their religious beliefs and in keeping more with Christian teachings. Their extreme expressions of religion include limiting and reversing women's rights. The religious right's move toward radical Christianity blurs the line between church and state. The religious right says change is necessary because the end of the world is near, as evidenced by wars in the Middle East, terrorism, and Jews settling in biblical Israel.

Some Americans think that the United States is creeping toward theocracy as religious values influence lawmaking on issues such as abortion. The conservative Republican majority has grown and is dominating politics. Its members believe they can restore order and stability to a society that has become increasingly chaotic.

FIGHTING THEOCRACY

Conflicts in the Middle East are based on differing ideals and beliefs, much as the American Civil War was undertaken against slavery. World War II and the Cold War were fought against fascism and communism. Today, conflicts and wars are being

The Palestinian group Islamic Jihad burns US flags in December 2017 in protest of US president Donald Trump's recognition of Jerusalem as the capital of Israel.

fought against groups such as the Taliban and ISIS, either to bring in theocracy or to banish it. In Iran, the religious and political revolution in 1979 made that country into an Islamic state. Theocratic Islamic groups are waging jihad against non-Muslims. They seek to suppress Western thought and to advance their religious beliefs through force and violence. Martyrdom plays a role in their expression of Islam.

JOHN ROBERT GALLAGHER

A Canadian from Calgary, John Robert Gallagher volunteered to fight against ISIS in northern Syria. On November 4, 2015, Gallagher was killed by gunfire, the first Canadian volunteer to die in battle. He was thirty-two years old. Gallagher had previously served there with Canadian forces and returned as a volunteer after retiring. He strongly believed in the importance of fighting ISIS because of its violation of human rights. Gallagher described why he volunteered to fight in the war in an essay published by the Toronto *National Post*. He wrote, “Theocracy isn't just as dangerous as fascism; it's the model of fascism, all totalitarianisms. Communism said ‘instead of God, the Party.’ Fascism said, ‘instead of God, the Nation!’ Theocracy simply says ‘God.’”

THEOCRACY IN LITERATURE

Theocracy has been often written about, from ancient times to the modern, from treatises of government to fiction. *The Handmaid's Tale* was published in 1985 by Margaret Atwood and then filmed as a television series. Set in a future Massachusetts, the novel draws on the theocratic beliefs of that state's early Puritans settlers. This work of fiction imagines a theocratic America without a president or Congress, where women are oppressed, and life is regulated and under constant watch. It presents a thought-provoking portrait of what theocracies in the modern age might hold.

TIMELINE

3000 BCE A central theocratic government forms in Egypt.

1920 BCE Yahweh is appointed the civil ruler of the Hebrew people.

1600 BCE The Shang dynasty in China functions as a theocracy.

1400 BCE A theocratic government comes to power in Egypt.

27 BCE Rome's emperors rule as theocratic heads of state.

100 CE Jewish historian Flavius Josephus coins the term "theocracy."

250 CE Aztec, Inca, and Maya civilizations establish strong theocracies.

350 CE The Roman Empire becomes a Christian state under Constantine the Great.

1509 John Calvin creates a theocratic Protestant state in Geneva, Switzerland.

1600 Theocracies decline during the Age of Enlightenment.

1620 The Pilgrims develop a theocracy in Plymouth, Massachusetts.

1630 The Puritans start a theocracy in Massachusetts Bay Colony.

1740s The first Saudi state establishes Islamic law.

1820s A Mormon theocracy is founded in New York State.

1872 The Jehovah's Witnesses are established in Pittsburgh, Pennsylvania.

1905 The Satmar Hasidic Jewish theocracy is founded in Hungary.

1929 Vatican City becomes an independent and theocratic state.

1959 Tibet forms a central theocratic state.

1979 Iran becomes a theocratic republic.

1989 The Christian Coalition is formed.

1996 The Taliban begins rule of Afghanistan until 2001.

***Antiquity of the Jews. Against Apion*, Book I, by Flavius Josephus (ca. 96–100 CE)**

Transcription Excerpt

"Our legislator [Moses] ... ordained our government to be what, by a strained expression, may be termed a theocracy, by ascribing the authority and power to God, and by persuading all people to have a regard to him, as the author of all good things enjoyed either in common by all mankind, or by each one in particular, and of all that they themselves obtained by praying to him in their greatest difficulties."

United States Constitution, Amendment 1 (December 15, 1791)

Transcription Excerpt

"Congress shall make no law respecting an establishment of religion, or prohibiting the free exercise thereof; or abridging the freedom of speech, or of the press; or the right of the people peaceably to assemble, and to petition the Government for a redress of grievances."

"We Are All on the Front Lines," ***National Post,*** **by John Robert Gallagher (November 5, 2015)**

Transcription Excerpt

"We are all on the front lines of this conflict, whether we know it or not. We can measure the casualties not only in the body counts of deadly terror attacks, mass demonstrations, embassy assaults and assassinated artists; we can also measure it in the terror produced among cartoonists, satirists, publishers and booksellers, news media and educators who are being prevented from doing their necessary work of maintaining the machinery of the enlightenment. Not only have we all been threatened; in many ways we are all already casualties of this war."

GLOSSARY

CANON LAW Church law, especially in Roman Catholicism.

CHADOR A covering worn by some Muslim women that only exposes the face or eyes.

CITY-STATE An independent state comprising a city and the surrounding territory.

CONSTITUTION Principles by which a country is governed.

DEITY A god or goddess or a supreme being.

DIVINE RIGHT The claim that the right to rule comes directly from God.

DYNASTY A line of rulers who inherit their leadership.

HIJAB A headscarf worn by some Muslim women.

JIHAD Declaring and waging war on the enemies of Islam.

LEGISLATIVE A lawmaking body and the making of laws.

ORACLE A person or object through which gods can communicate.

PATENT A license that grants government authority.

POLYGAMY Having more than one spouse at a time.

POLYTHEISM The belief in and worship of many gods.

REPUBLIC A government of the people and their elected representatives.

SECULAR Any activity or attitude without religious basis.

SHARIA Islamic religious laws based on the Quran.

TALIBAN An Islamic religious movement.

THEODEMOCRACY A theocracy with elements of democracy.

FOR MORE INFORMATION

Americans United for Separation of Church and State
1310 L Street NW, Suite 200
Washington, DC 20005
(202) 466-3234
Website: http://www.au.org
Facebook, Twitter, and Instagram: @americansunited
This organization advocates for the separation of church and state on issues such as reproductive and LGBTQ rights, religious freedom, and religious discrimination.

Canadian Museum of History
100 Laurier Street
Gatineau, QC KIA 0M8
Canada
(800) 555-5621
Website: https://www.historymuseum.ca
Facebook, Twitter, and Instagram: @CanMusHistory
The museum offers exhibits and online resources about ancient Egypt and its rulers and religion, as well as information on the early Greek and Maya civilizations.

Metropolitan Museum of Art
1000 Fifth Avenue
New York, NY 10028
(212) 535-7710
Website: https://www.metmuseum.org
Facebook, Twitter, and Instagram: @metmuseum
As the largest museum in the United States, the Met has a significant collection of art and religious and household items dating from Egypt's earliest days. Also displayed are items

from ancient Greece and Rome and from Arab countries such as Iran.

Museum of Muslim Cultures
201 East Pascagoula Street
Jackson, MS 39201
(601) 960-0440
Website: http://www.muslimmuseum.org
Facebook and Twitter: @muslimmuseum
Through exhibits and education, the museum broadens knowledge about the culture and history of Muslims worldwide.

Political Research Associates (PRA)
1310 Broadway, Suite 201
Somerville, MA 02144
(617) 666-5300
Website: http://www.politicalresearch.org
Facebook: @PoliticalResearchAssociates
Twitter: @PRAEyesRight
A think tank, the PRA educates and studies the US right wing versus secular positions on several issues, including race, immigration, and civil liberties.

Religious Tolerance
Ontario Consultants on Religious Tolerance (OCRT)
PO Box 128
Watertown, NY 13601
(888) 806-6115
Website: https://www.religioustolerance.org
Facebook: @religioustolerance
Twitter: @ReligiousTol
Based in Canada, this multifaith website promotes religious tolerance. Although not associated with any one religion, the

website posts objective discussions and essays on the different world religions, including theocracies.

TheocracyWatch
Center for Religion, Ethics, and Social Policy (CRESP)
Cornell University
Ithaca, NY 14853
(607) 254-4636
Website: http://www.theocracywatch.org
A project run by CRESP, this website offers discussions and videos that monitor the influence of dominionism and the Christian right's influence on American society.

FOR FURTHER READING

Atwood, Margaret. *The Handmaid's Tale*. New York, NY: Anchor Books, 1998.

Berlatsky, Noah. *The Taliban*. Detroit, MI: Greenhaven Press, 2011.

Boyle, Sarah B. *What Is a Theocracy?* New York, NY: Crabtree Publishing Company, 2013.

Connolly, Sean. *Fundamentalism*. London, UK: Wayland, 2014.

Connolly, Sean. *Systems of Government: Theocracy*. London, UK: Hachette Kids Franklin Watts, 2017.

Davidson, Tish. *Theocracy*. Broomall, PA: Mason Crest, 2013.

Keppeler, Jill. *Ancient Maya Government*. New York, NY: Rosen Publishing, 2017.

Lucerne, Sam. *Theocracies*. Edina, MN: ABDO Publishing, 2011.

Marsh, Corinda. *Salem's Theocracy: Shattered on the Rock of Witchcraft*. Charleston, SC: CreateSpace Independent, 2016.

Rodgers, Kelly. *The New England Colonies: A Place for Puritans*. Huntington Beach, CA: Teacher Created Materials, 2017.

Anonymous Parent. "Raising Children in a Theocracy: Anonymous Parent Shares Personal Story of Living in Rabun County, Georgia." TheHumanist.com, September 14, 2015. https://thehumanist.com/features/articles/raising-children-in-a-theocracy-anonymous-parent-shares-personal-story-of-living-in-rabun-county-georgia.

Bills of Rights in Action. "Puritan Massachusetts: Theocracy or Democracy?" Constitutional Rights Foundation, Fall 2013, vol. 29, no. 1. http://www.crf-usa.org/images/pdf/gates/puritans-of-mass.pdf.

Bruton, F. Brinley, and Paul Goldman. "Israel's Government Could Fall Over Ultra-Orthodox Enlistment." NBC News, March 6, 2018. https://www.nbcnews.com/news/world/amp/Israel-s-government-could-fall-over-ultra-orthodox-enlistment-n853556.

Evans, Maxwell. "MSU Student, Lansing Resident Share Their Lives Under a Theocracy in Iran." *State News*, November 2, 2017. http://statenews.com/article/2017/11/iranian-bahai-headline.

Fiske, John. *The Beginnings of New England: Or the Puritan Theocracy in Its Relations to Civil and Religious Liberty*. New York, NY: Firework Press, 2015.

Forseter, Murray. "The Sad Movement Toward Theocracies in America and Israel." Huffington Post, June 26, 2017. https://www.huffingtonpost.com/entry/the-sad-movement-toward-theocracies-in-america-and_us_5951b1dde4b0326c0a8d0ae2.

Hamilton, Marci. "The History of Religion in the United States: Liberty and Theocracy." *Constitution Daily*, National Constitution Center, September 14, 2015. https://

constitutioncenter.org/blog/the-history-of-religion-in-the-united-states-liberty-and-theocracy.

Myers, David N., and Nomi M. Stolzenberg. "Kiryas Joel: Theocracy in America?" Huffington Post, February 3, 2012. https://www.huffingtonpost.com/entry/kiryas-yoel-theocracy-in-america_b_1124505.

Rampell, Catherine. "Christians Pushing Theocracy in America." *Billings Gazette*, February 6, 2017. http://billingsgazette.com/opinion/columnists/catherine-rampell-christians-pushing-theocracy-in-america/article_5da656fc-3c5f-5b73-8ca6-5f7ced147b93.html.

Shelley, Fred M., ed. *Governments Around the World: From Democracies to Theocracies*. Santa Barbara, CA: ABC-CLIO, 2015.

Tayler, Jeffrey. "They Really Want a Theocracy: The GOP Candidates Who Want to Make You Bow to Their Lord." Salon.com, October 25, 2015. https://www.salon.com/2015/10/25/they_really_want_a_theocracy_the_gop_candidates_who_want_to_make_you_bow_to_their_lord.

Theroux, David J. "Secular Theocracy: The Foundations and Folly of Modern Tyranny." Independent Institute, January 11, 2012. http://www.independent.org/publications/article.asp?id=3206.

Werleman, C. J. "We Are a Corporate Theocracy Now: The Christian Right Seeks Cultural and Political Domination." Salon.com, July 3, 2014. https://www.salon.com/2014/07/03/we_are_a_corporate_theocracy_now_the_christian_right_seeks_cultural_and_political_domination.

INDEX

ABOUT THE AUTHOR

Henrietta Toth is a writer and editor with twenty years of experience in academic publishing. She has worked on books about business, economics, history, law, public policy, religion, and social justice. She enjoys reading about world history and writing about it for children and young adults.

PHOTO CREDITS

Cover (Pope Francis) Giulio Napolitano/Shutterstock.com; cover (Bible) Stephen Orsillo/Shutterstock.com; cover (Tarawih prayer) Barcroft Media/Getty Images; p. 5 Ahmad Al-Rubaye/AFP /Getty Images; p. 7 Mondadori Portfolio/Hulton Fine Art Collection/Getty Images; p. 11 Los Angeles County Museum of Art, The Madina Collection of Islamic Art, gift of Camilla Chandler Frost; p. 12 Grigvovan/Shutterstock.com; p. 16 WitR /Shutterstock.com; p. 17 Kelsey Green/Shutterstock.com; p. 20 Fabrice Coffrini/AFP/Getty Images; pp. 23, 39 AFP/Getty Images; p. 25 Mikhail Markovskiy/Shutterstock.com; p. 26 Heritage Images/Hulton Archive/Getty Images; p. 29 © North Wind Picture Archives; p. 31 American Antiquarian Society, Worcester, Massachusetts, USA/Bequest of William Winthrop /Bridgeman Images; p. 33 The Metropolitan Museum of Art, Gilman Collection, Purchase, Marlene Nathan Meyerson Family Foundation Gift, 2005; p. 37 Robert Nickelsberg/Gamma-Rapho /Getty Images; p. 41 NurPhoto/Getty Images; p. 43 Kaveh Kazemi /Hulton Archive/Getty Images; p. 45 Gil Cohen-Magen/AFP /Getty Images; p. 47 National Archives; p. 49 Mohammed Abed /AFP/Getty Images; chapter opener pages (world map silhouette) Vectorios2016/DigitalVision Vectors/Getty Images.

Design and Layout: Nicole Russo-Duca; Photo Researcher: Nicole DiMella